Brooke's Journey

Life, loss and healing

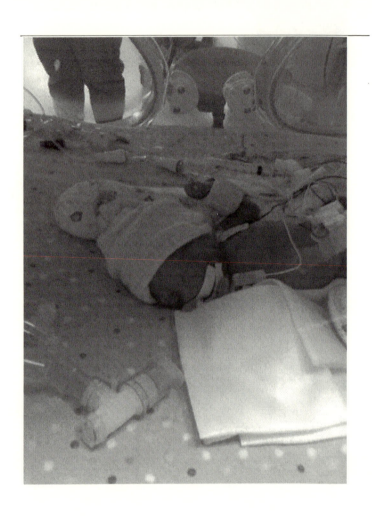

We don't always understand the ways of God and when little Brooke was born prematurely to Scott and Becky Becker, this was one of those times. There were times of pleading with God for Brooke's survival followed by little signs of improvement that brought a ray of hope. Finally, however, God chose to take that little life to Himself. It followed that her few days on earth were a spiritual journey for her parents. Throughout this journey, Scott kept in touch with his church family, First Baptist of St. Johns, Michigan. This book is really Scott's heart-wrenching,heartwarming experience as they awaited God's answer to their prayers. Experiences of hardship and sorrow refine faith so that, though brief, Brooke's life had a lasting legacy. During her pregnancy, Becky thought that she was carrying this baby much lower than her former pregnancies. After Brooke's birth it was discovered this "lower than usual" pregnancy was really a large, benign tumor. In a sense, Brooke's premature birth saved her mother's life. God's Word tells us that His ways are higher than our ways and His thoughts than our thoughts, and so we must learn to trust Him in every experience of life. May Scott and Becky's account of their journey encourage the reader to trust our loving Father also.

    —Frances D. Nelson

"Life is what happens to us while we're making other plans." *This line has stuck with me since my mother-in-law passed away in 2000 as the result of a bike accident. Tragedies, and deaths in particular, have a way of getting our attention and reminding us that we are not autonomous.*

My wife Becky and I were married in 1984. We had decided we would "take" as many children as God would give us. Those were our plans. After seven years we were childless. After unsuccessfully working with a fertility specialist, we were told we would probably never have children of our own. God had other plans.

In 1992, God blessed us with a daughter. In 1997, He blessed us with another daughter. In 2000, He blessed us with a third daughter. In 2004, God decided to smile upon us once again and bless us with a son. A very special child with an extra chromosome. A child with Down's Syndrome was not on our radar, but God knew what He was doing. But that is another story.

We assumed God was done blessing us with children of our own. Our daughters assumed we were too old to have more children and began "pressuring" us to adopt. In the middle or our plans, "life" happened to us. In late 2009 we were expecting again, with a due date in June of 2010. On February 10th of 2010, my wife's water broke. Before we even had our belts fastened, the chains started to rattle and the coaster started to ascend the first hill. Who knew what kind of ride we were in for?

Just before midnight on February 18th, my wife started contractions. We knew the baby was just shy of being deemed viable being less than twenty-three weeks. Accordingly, we knew we were probably going to be faced with some difficult decisions. At least we were going to be making them as a team. Or so I thought. When we arrived at the hospital, we were confronted by a nurse who did not believe our "story" and seemed in no hurry to get us help. Another nurse overheard our conversation and took charge. She actually knew our names and our story as she heard about our situation at church and was praying for us. Talk about a guardian angel! She immediately got us into a room. Things were developing very quickly, unfortunately the Doctor who was supposed to do the delivery could not be reached. A very capable team was assembled and at 3:30 a.m. our fourth daughter, Brooke Elizabeth was born weighing in at 1lb, 8oz. A NICU team was waiting outside the door and our precious little bundle was immediately whisked away to be tended to. How quickly the coaster was approaching the first peak. The delivery happened so quickly that the incubator wasn't sufficiently heated. There were early concerns that Brooke may need to have a leg amputated. Before we had time to process the information coming at us, we were "blindsided". Hours after delivery, my wife was fighting for her own life. Instead of making decisions with my spouse for our daughter, I was faced with making decisions for my wife and daughter who were both in intensive care. Unknown to us, my wife had a football sized tumor on one of her kidneys. Attached to this tumor were three aneurysms which burst after delivery. The Doctor who was supposed to deliver Brooke "happened" to check in on my wife and determined that she was bleeding internally. He immediately called for blood. It would take 17 units in less than 24 hours just to enable the surgery to be done removing the tumor and the kidney it encapsulated. Amazing how fast a roller coaster moves. In time, my wife fully recovered. After she was home a friend from church, Pam, delivered a meal and shared with us that a lot of people from church were faithfully praying for Brooke just as they did for my wife, and would like to be kept updated on her condition. We decided that because of time constraints, I would send updates to Pam, and she would "edit" and forward to the church family and other interested parties. What follows are those e-mails. I share this background information to put things in context and to explain the gap between

Brooke's birth and the first e-mail. As you ride along, may you be encouraged to enjoy the life that happens to you as you are making other plans. As you're making plans, don't forget God.

"Come now, you who say, 'Today or tomorrow we will go into such and such a town and spend a year there and trade and make a profit' - yet you do not know what tomorrow will bring. What is your life? For you are a mist that appears for a little time and then vanishes. Instead you ought to say, 'If the Lord wills, we will live and do this or that."

James 4:13-15

Mon, Mar 8, 2010 at 6:47 PM

Pam,

I Wanted to let you know Brooke's status. Brooke continues to have lung and kidney issues. She has not responded the way they had hoped. They put a tube in her chest (again) to alleviate the "air" problem. She is not exchanging it on her own. Dr. K. re-emphasized again today that she cannot continue to have these set-backs and ensuing procedures. It appears that they are giving up on Brooke and I feel like they are thinking we should do the same. I reminded them that we would like to keep fighting as long as there is even the faintest glimmer of hope. At the same time, we want to be "fair" to Brooke. The staff is placing great emphasis on today's procedure with the chest tube. It is critical that Brooke responds positively and has a few good days or they will really be pressuring us.

Thanks for your prayers.

Scott

Mar 9, 2010 at 7:02 AM

Pam,

I just talked to Brooke's night nurse. Brooke had a very good night. They were able to lower the oxygen pressure and she urinated a lot. According to the nurse it was a step forward without a step back. We need to see Brooke maintain this "momentum" which seems to be her difficulty.

I appreciate all the prayers and support. Our peace comes from knowing that God loves Brooke even more than we do, and He doesn't make mistakes.

Thanks for everything.

Scott

Thu, Mar 11, 2010 at 7:07 AM

Pam,

When I got to the hospital last night the nurse said Brooke had a "very good" day. I called early this morning and the nurse said Brooke is "cruising". Thanks for all the prayers. It is very important that Brooke's lung situation stabilizes because she has stomach issues that need to be addressed but have been ignored because of her lungs. Hopefully Brooke keeps "cruising".

Thanks again for everything. I will try to keep you updated. I know people are looking to you for updates so this system helps me a lot.

God Bless,

Scott

Thu, March 11, 2010 at 9:04 AM

Dear praying Friends,

I wanted to let you know that we are going to be meeting for prayer every Wednesday from 12-12:30 p.m. in the church sanctuary for Brooke until the day the Lord heals her and Scott and Becky bring her home. Everyone is welcome!
Pam

Psalm 46:10

Thu, Mar 11, 2010 at 12:48 PM

Pam,

They have just removed one of the chest tubes (still 2 remaining). They are now concentrating on stomach issue. They x-rayed the stomach and will have results later today. I will keep you posted as I learn more. Need to pray that lungs co-operate this time and do not collapse again.

Thanks,

Scott

March 15th 2010 at 10:52 AM

Pam,

Brooke had a very good night. The night nurse decided to "clean" the cath. and found that it was plugged!! I specifically asked the nurse yesterday if that was a possibility and she laughed at me (urgh). Brooke has urinated throughout the night and her swelling has gone down some. Audrey (Brooke's nurse) even got her oxygen down to 22 (21 is perfect). You may want to thank God for Audrey. She is the nurse that was caring for Brooke when she first opened her eyes and "her heart melted". According to her peers Audrey has a special place in her heart for Brooke. Audrey asked to work exclusively with Brooke. Every evening she works; she only sees Brooke. This consistency means a lot to Mom & Dad.

We have not personally met her but we enjoy talking with her and have great confidence in her. I have been able to thank her for "adopting" Brooke, but that feels so inadequate.

Forgive the disjointedness of this e-mail. Dad is needing sleep. I am trusting you to "make me look good" as you forward this rambling. Trusting you are a good editor. Thanks again,

Scott

Monday March 15 2010

Dear Praying Friends,

The time has come for us to pray as never before for Scott and Becky and their family. The doctors have told them that precious Brooke is too weak, too tiny and too sick to fight any more. With this information they have decided not to allow the doctors to perform any more "heroic efforts" to keep her alive. The family now waits on the Lord as he finishes her mansion and prepares to bring her back home. They covet your prayers for strength and peace at this time. Pam...for the Becker family

Tuesday March 16, 2010

Pam,

Do you like roller coaster rides? I called the hospital at 5:30 a.m. & 11:00 a.m. yesterday and was told that Brooke was having a good morning which followed a good night Sunday. At 3:00 p.m. I got a call from the hospital saying that Brooke's stats were dropping and there was nothing more they could do for her. Beck & I met with Dr. K. & 3 nurses and they implied that Brooke's got little to no hope. We did not like the "no" so we are embracing the "little". We do not mean any disrespect to their professional experience, but we are not at peace with quitting. We mutually agreed to back off of the aggressive care and to see if Brooke does a little more on her own. Besides, they are running out of places to poke her. They expressed great concern that Brooke is becoming less tolerant of being handled. Her heart rate dropped as low as 60 which is the equivalent of 0 for an adult and requires resuscitation. We chose not to hold her at this time or to say good-bye. I was able to kiss her and tell her I love her and tell her I am sorry for all she has been through. When she looks at you with those precious eyes you cannot quit!!!!

I called Audrey last night before bed and again at 5:00 this morning and she informed me that Brooke's heart rate was back in the 140's and her stats were good again. As a matter of fact, she had her eyes open a lot and was working over her pacifier. Remember one of the main reasons they thought we should stop the fight was that Brooke had become so lethargic! Beck & I went to the hospital this morning and Brooke's stats were still strong. We had a good visit and were able to leave her an I-Pod so she has music (per request of the nurses not Brooke). I called back at 3:00 to follow up since things seem to change so fast.

Brooke's stats are still strong and she even gave us a surprise; a little "poop" in her diaper. Further proof that every bathroom should have music piped in.

I find it interesting that they have told us there is nothing more "they" can do. If little Brooke is going to come home it has to be entirely of God!! I don't mean to set out a fleece but what might the impact be if God were to grace us with a miracle to be witnessed by so many? If it is going to happen He is going to allow us to be a part of it, which means more prayer. We need to specifically pray for Brooke's kidneys, lungs, liver and digestive system. Her needs seem insurmountable, but God is the "Great Physician". We are growing weary of the ride, but we do not want it to end. Brace yourself and hold tight (to the cross).

Scott

Wed, March 17, 2010 at 11:38 AM

Pam,

Just got back from the hospital and wanted to give you the most current info for your prayer time. Brooke had a good night and morning "playing" with Audrey. They truly have a special relationship. Brooke had a couple more BM's so you could say Audrey brings out the best in Brooke (well sort of). Stats are still good. Brooke passed 80 cc's of urine during Audrey's shift and was still passing some when I was up there so that is encouraging. Brooke seems to like the swabbing of breast milk they are now giving her around her mouth. Mom and dad consider this a great victory as they were reluctant to introduce the milk to Brooke at this time. Brooke's bloated appearance has gone down substantially, I did not mistake her for a substantially older preemie today.

We need to continue in earnest prayer for her kidney to maintain, for her liver to show signs of working, for her air exchange to improve and for her digestive system to continue to show signs of being operational. Also, Audrey informed me this morning that she will be off for a week (ouch). Brooke definitely responds best to her adopted mother and I have concerns about her absence. I recognize that God is ultimately in control but for some reason most of His miracles have happened through Audrey. Maybe dad needs to be weaned from his reliance on Audrey? Thanks again for everything.

Scott

Thu, March 18, 2010 at 8:48 AM

Good morning Pam,

Are you growing weary yet? I didn't realize when we started how wide our circulation would be. I'm sure the NY Times would be jealous. In all honesty I'm humbled by the number of people that are following Brooke's journey. I'm confident it is only the prayers being lifted for us that are keeping us going. Since that is true we will carry on (with requests). As of 6:00 a.m. this morning Brooke's stats are still good. This includes her heart rate (around 130), her saturation rate (around 90) and her oxygen level (around 35). Per Jamie, her nurse for last night's shift, Brooke put out 76 c.c.'s of urine. I originally took this to be good news but apparently they are concerned that now she is "going too much". Her sodium levels are rising and there are electrolyte issues. Now I know why I do taxes!! I can no longer differentiate between good news and bad. Jamie told me that despite the urine "flow" of the past few days, Brooke is still considered to have renal failure. She has 2 counts (B.U.N. & creatine(I think) that are off of the charts and rising. I don't mean to get too technical but it does help for more specific prayer. The B.U.N.

count is 115, normal is 5-15. The creatine (?) is 3.88 and should be 0-.5. These counts are very troubling to the Dr's and nurses, so I decided to "trouble" everyone else with them. Thanks again to everyone for the outpouring of love & support. May God be glorified in all of our lives, and may everyone experience increased faith as we petition our Abba Father.

God Bless,

Scott (For Brooke & her family)

Thursday March 18, 2010 #2 (P.M.)

Pam,

Just wanted to shoot you a quick praise. I got home from the hospital around 5:00 and Brooke is having a really good day. Her stats are good. B.U.N. & creatinine (breaks down creatine) are down slightly. Privacy partitions with "quiet" signs that have been surrounding Brooke were taken down (she's becoming more sociable). I hope this means they are expecting her to stay around for a while. Brooke's nurse Connie, was actually out in the hallway doing some miscellaneous cleaning (a new dome for Brooke).

Usually the nurses are laboring over Brooke. Brooke was sleeping so peacefully. They even lowered her morphine. Brooke is still urinating, and Connie said she heard some belly rumblings which is a very good sign. Connie was actually going to give Brooke a bath since she is having such a good day. I was not going to go to the hospital today because I have been rather exhausted. What a blessing I would have missed. Connie referred to Brooke as the Energizer Bunny. Every time they think she is "finished", she comes bouncing back. That statement certainly energized me!! I want to be careful not to get "too high" knowing how quickly things can turn, but as I like to tell the Dr's & nurses when Brooke is having a good day: It sure beats the alternative. By the way: tomorrow morning at 3:30 is Brooke's 1-month birthday. Praise God for His Blessings and His mercy. He truly has been so good to us.

Thanks again for all the prayers.
Brooke's proud father
Scott

March 19, 2010

Pam,

Dad (your's truly) could not sleep last night, apparently suffering from excited-itis. Today is the big 1 month birthday!!! As I lay in bed last night my mind replayed many of the events of the past month. Life certainly is full of ironies. If I had my choice I would not have asked for the "trials" we have faced, and yet looking back I would not trade them. God has shown His faithfulness and demonstrated His sovereignty in so many ways. The outpouring of support has *been incredible and extremely humbling. We feel so unworthy.*

I decided not to share any specific prayer requests today. I want to soak in the joy of this milestone for Brooke by praising her true Father. I realize that our prayers are not a burden to God, but I believe from time to time it is good for us to pause and contemplate His faithfulness and the many blessings He bestows upon us. I want to thank everyone for the food, gas cards, firewood, cleaning, babysitting, hospitality, etc. More importantly I want to thank everyone for praying. There are people from so many different faiths uniting to pray for

Brooke; again we are humbled by the support. I thank you all for being God's "hands & feet". I do not believe that thanking you robs from God because He works through you!!

Please take time out today to Thank God for who He is. Let Him know how much you appreciate what He means to you. Give your loved ones a hug and tell them that you love them. We don't know how many chances we will have. Eat some cake & ice cream.

Happy birthday Brooke. Thank you God for such a great "gift". Thank all of you again for being such a big part of this milestone!! Hoping some of you have caught the "excited-itits".

Dad, for birthday girl

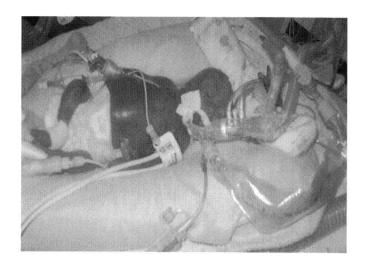

SATURDAY MARCH 20, 2010

Pam,

What a treat it was too see Brooke with her little pink bow on her Birthday, although I think the significance of the occasion was lost on her. For the most part she slept during the entire visit with mom & dad. Some children just show no respect for their parents!

Brooke's stats have remained fairly stable which is a great relief. Her B.U.N. count is still high, but her creatinine is coming down slightly. They are checking Brooke for a possible heart murmur and have done an ultrasound on her brain (looking for hemorrhages). Please pray that results are negative.

Brooke's lungs appear to be fully expanded; unfortunately they seem to be full of fluids. Not sure when the chest tube will be coming out.

Urination seems to be slowing down, please pray that she doesn't pull her typical "I'm taking the weekend off" from peeing. She can be so stubborn sometimes. She obviously gets that from Mom.

Brooke's belly still looks very large and dusky looking. The Dr's say that her liver is extremely enlarged and taking up a lot of space.

I realize I have given you a lot of (negative) info. Please forgive me if it is too much detail. We knew from the beginning that Brooke would have an "uphill" battle; I never could have imagined just how steep the hill would be. I believe that it is through prayer power that Brooke will be able to conquer her hill. She is too "weak" to make the climb alone, but God is gracious in allowing us to help carry her in prayer. We are "strongest" when on our knees. God allowed Caleb to conquer his hill as an old man, may He allow our preemie to do the same.

We keep marching on. God is glorified as we grow and walk (up the hill) in faith.

Thanks to everyone for praying, and thanks to the nurses for Brooke's bath & bow. If you're going to conquer a hill you deserve to do it looking your best!!

God Bless,

Scott

Sun, March 21, 2010 at 12:08 PM

Pam,

I went to visit Brooke yesterday afternoon. I got to Brooke's room (otherwise known as the pink room) around 3:30 and went to the sink nearest Brooke for my mandatory 3 minute washing. I noticed a lady that I did not recognize on the other side of Brooke's isolate and she seemed a little distressed. I immediately felt my blood pressure rising. As she was intently looking at the beeping monitor she picked up a "hammer" and began tapping Brooke's chest. I began to feel a little faint! Next she began squeezing some "bag". They had told us that when they resuscitate a preemie they use "bags". The 3 minute timer could not seem slower as time seemed to stand still. After the squeezing procedure the "lady" then grabbed a syringe. I could not understand why none of the other staff was coming to assist my fading daughter. Finally, my timer (a mini-hour glass) was up, I quickly dried my arms and hands (I'm surprised I didn't wash my toes) and walked around the isolette and asked the lady if she was having troubles. She smiled at me and said "Brooke's having a good day." Do you think dad's stress level is high?

This stranger was actually Brooke's nurse Burt (Rachel thinks it's short for Burtrude). The hammer was an innocent rubber utensil used to break up the fluids in Brooke's lungs so that the lungs could then be cleaned via extraction with the "bag". Did I feel stupid. Hopefully Burt did not recognize my concern. Pale fathers are probably common in the NICU!? True story. Thought you could use a good laugh at my expense. Brooke's stats remain good. The echo did show a heart murmur (the PDA has re-

opened). I think this is fairly common, and Burt did not seem too concerned.

The brain ultrasound came back negative, no hemorrhages!!! Very good news. Brooke's color looked as good as it has in quite some time. I'm hoping this means something positive in relationship to her liver as she was a little brownish. Brooke's B.U.N. and creatinine remain high. Her kidneys still seem to be the major concern right now. She had very little urine yesterday, but Burt did change Brooke's diaper when I was there and she did urinate around the cath. She has not completely stopped like she did last weekend. Beck called the hospital this *morning and it appears that Brooke has some free air in her stomach? Not sure what this means but I will let you know as I know more.*

Scott

Mon, March 22, 2010 at 11:53 AM

Pam,

I had a long talk with Brooke's nurse this morning (6:15 a.m). Brooke kicked out her cath. and started to urinate quite a bit. Stats were good, etc. Thought we were on the right track.

Just (10:00 am) received a call from another nurse wanting to know what we were told this morning? I asked if Brooke was ok and the nurse was pretty evasive. They would like Beck & I to come up for a meeting this afternoon. I cringe to think of what they might say and the pressure they may put on us to give up the fight.

Please pray for wisdom, courage & peace. We truly want to do what is best for Brooke. I don't want to fight for the wrong reasons or to be blinded by emotions.

Appreciate all the prayer support we can get for this meeting.

Scott

Mon, March 22, 2010 at 6:20 PM

Second Monday update

Pam,

It appears we are in need of another "miracle". Brooke just had a tube put back into her abdomen to relieve building pressure. She had this procedure a few weeks back for her perforated intestine. Dr. J., who did the procedure, said it is very rare to have to do it twice. He believes that the cortisone Brooke is on "retarded' the healing process. Per Dr. J., Brooke is "hanging on by a thread". It is possible Brooke could need intestinal surgery, which they feel she could not survive because of her health. They are also afraid of infection, which could be fatal, because her kidneys will not tolerate the necessary antibiotic.

-If you have any "special" kidney or anti-infection prayers, now would be the time to bring them out!!

Also, please pray for Dr. K. & the staff. As we stood over Brooke's isolette after the surgery, Dr. K. & the nurses present were misty eyed as we talked about Brooke and the plans going forward. I was able to thank them for their diligence and care for Brooke. I recognize that because of her fragile condition they are very limited in what they are able to do for Brooke. I appreciate what they have done thus far with their "hands tied".

We have really grown to love Brooke's team. They are very special people who give their all, and as they have told us, "go home exhausted". It is obvious that they have grown fond of Brooke which makes us feel good as parents!!! Thanking God for His Grace, as we wait for another miracle.
Scott

Tue, March 23, 2010 2:43 PM

Pam,

I called up to the hospital around 11:00 am. Brooke apparently has stopped urinating again. Her basic stats are pretty good but the B.U.N & creatinine continue to climb as she stops urinating, which really limits what the Dr's are able to do for her. It appears that the tube they put in yesterday to alleviate the pressure in her stomach is plugged. Hopefully this will be an easy fix. I was encouraged by the nurse (Laura). She said she is praying for Brooke. It is so humbling to hear this from the nurses. It always brings tears to my eyes to experience such care & compassion from the "professionals". Many of them recognize that they are merely tools in God's hands. The other important quote from Laura re: Brooke "She is so stinking cute". A proud father couldn't help but share that important piece of info!!! Thanks again for everything.

Scott

Thu, Mar 25, 2010 at 11:01 AM

Pam,

Just wanted to let you know that Brooke had a difficult day yesterday. Her oxygen levels were all over the place and she was very restless. Brooke has been taken off of the ventilator and put back on the oscillator. Not a good sign. The ventilator was not able to adequately meet Brooke's needs. The oscillator is the end of the line, there is nothing "stronger". Brooke produced very little urine yesterday (4c.c.'s), but last night seemed to be better (24c.c.'s).

When we got to the hospital last night they were giving Brooke an enema. The Dr. who put the tube in for the intestinal perforation wanted to know what was in Brooke's "system". Apparently nothing!

Our latest angel, Laura, the nurse who has had Brooke the last two days, commented that Brooke seemed more relaxed with mom & dad there. Can you say convicting? Because of Beck's health since her surgery, she has had to limit her visits with Brooke to 2 or 3 times a week. I am there every day, but because it is tax season, and because the nurses are so busy with Brooke, I limit my stays. There will be changes!!

As I looked at Brooke last night, in all of her discomfort and restlessness, my heart really ached. I so badly wanted to hold her and give her a "papa" bear "embrace" and assure her everything would be o.k. I've thought a lot about the way God has "wired" us as relational beings. Who can understand the soul? How does little Brooke sense the security of her parents? Does she "feel" our love? Just as I was tempted to ask the question "why does she have to endure this?" God impressed upon me His desire to express His love and to be loved in return.

This lump of clay was tempted to question the Potter (feel sorry for myself and Brooke). As I shared many years ago in a sermon, it is the love of God that helps us to accept His sovereignty. As he turns us on the potter's wheel and shapes us into the image of His Son, we can feel the nail marks in His hands. The cross is sufficient for me. Instead of questioning God, I need to let His love flow through me.

I thank God I was able to kiss Brooke last night. It is not the same as an embrace but I trust that she "feels" the love as our

souls unite. My prayer for today is that when I visit her she may feel the love and security of God. After all, He is the one that has created and is forming Brooke. Big Lump of clay for cute little lump of clay. Both in the Potter's hands.
Scott.

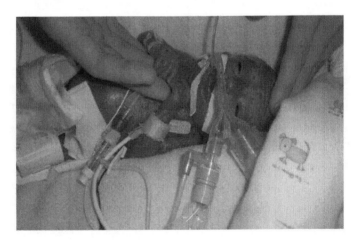

Fri, Mar 26, 2010 at 4:20 PM

Pam,

The meeting today was extremely difficult. The staff collectively told us that Brooke "has no chance". In all of their experience they have never seen symptoms such as Brooke's reverse. According to them she has not one but three fatal issues (kidneys, liver & lungs). Not to mention her digestive and heart concerns.

To me, Brooke looked better than she has in quite some time. Her color has improved, the swelling is down and she appears more "content". As I have said before, it is so hard to look into her eyes and quit. I feel like we are letting her down. I feel so helpless. It was difficult to walk out of her room and leave her there.

Please pray for wisdom for us. We did not make any decisions today, but we know we will need to after much prayer. We are so thankful for the 5 weeks we have had with Brooke and certainly were looking forward to bringing her home. If God chooses to call her Home first, may we graciously accept His will.

Please keep the girls in your prayers. Even before this pregnancy they have been asking us to adopt a child (didn't realize their parents could still have their own). They really have been excited about another baby in the house. This news is obviously devastating to them. I recognize we can't protect our loved ones from everything, but I pray that they will respond in a way that eventually strengthens their faith and is God honoring. Thanks again for everything.

Scott

P.S. You may want to pray for the NICU staff. I'm sure that delivering this news was not easy for them and these busy people cleared time to share from their hearts with us. Delivering this news probably wasn't much more enjoyable than receiving it. Also, many of these people have spent much more time with Brooke than we have and are very attached to her.

Saturday, March 27, 2010

Pam,

In yesterday's e-mail I mentioned how difficult it was to leave Brooke's room feeling like we had failed her. I would like to share with you the great experience we had today.

We arrived at Sparrow, as a family around 10:00 a.m. We took turns visiting with Brooke in her isolette for roughly a couple of hours. After some discussion, we decided to remove Brooke from the oscillator and put her back on the ventilator. This was done so that Brooke could be moved.

While we went out for a quick lunch, arrangements were made to allow us into a "family" room down the hall from "Brooke's room". After 5 weeks, all 7 of us were finally able to spend time together. The real blessing came when we were able to hold our daughter for the first time. Needless to say the tears flowed as I finally got to see Beck hold Brooke. I'm not sure how to describe it but I felt as if a very large burden was lifted from me. I'm not sure when I have ever been so happy for two very special people.

When Beck handed Brooke to me I expected to melt right into the chair. To the contrary I felt very invigorated. To finally be able to hold Brooke was an incredible balm for my aching heart. I'm not sure that this will make any sense, but somehow the ability to hold Brooke will make it easier to "let her go".

We stayed in the family room until 5:00 p.m. After everyone had a chance to hold Brooke, Beck held her for the duration of the time. It was such a thrill to see them bond the way God created them to. Despite her critical condition,

Brooke's stats never wavered the entire 7 hours.

We called the hospital this evening and Brooke is "no worse for the wear" so we are planning another family time tomorrow. Our intention is to invite grandparents and aunts and uncles.

We've already warned the hospital that they are a rough bunch, but they are willing to accommodate us anyhow. I am looking forward to "showing off" my precious daughter.

I realize that this is not the same as bringing Brooke home, but we are so grateful for the memories (and numerous pictures) of this very special day.

Seizing (and cherishing) each moment.

Scott

Mon, March 29, 2010 at 10:11 AM

Pam,

As you are well aware, at 3:41 p.m. yesterday afternoon, Brooke's "roller coaster" ride came to an end. She has passed from the shadowlands and into reality. She will know no more morphine. No more needles. No more transfusions & surgeries, ventilators or monitors. All of these things have been exchanged for the presence of her Savior. Gone are sin's consequences. In their place are the rewards of the Cross. No wonder they call it the "Great Exchange". I shared with the girls that as Christians we do not say good-bye, but rather "see ya on the other side.' Brooke is now on the other side and what joy she must be experiencing. Before her departure we were able to hold her again.

Grandparents, aunts, uncles and cousins were able to come into the "family room" and see Brooke on this side. Her heart rate continually dropped throughout the day. As the end of her ride was approaching I was able to hold her one last time. While she was in my arms she pushed the tubes out of her mouth. I praise God that He used Brooke to show us the end. He spared us from making that painful decision.

For Brooke the ride is over, but for us it still goes on. The swing set and trampoline in the backyard and the rocking chair by the fireplace are reminders that we must painfully say goodbye to our dreams and plans of raising Brooke. Instead we will have a tombstone just outside our front door. This does not "feel" like a great exchange to those of us still in the shadowlands. I tell you this not because we want your pity, but because we still covet your prayers. There will be no going back to life as normal, because "normal" has been re-defined. Being molded is never easy, but always worth it. I have been asked a lot of questions about heaven. The speculation is that Beck's mother is now holding our daughter before the face of our Heavenly Father. We envision Him saying "Welcome home my feisty little girl". I doubt that this is accurate. I'm confident that reality is even better than we can speculate from the shadowlands. I'm sure that their bliss is greater than words can describe. I'm thankful that this world is not our home!

We love you Brooke. We're sorry that all you ever knew on this earth was pain and suffering. Thank you for sharing your ride with us and making us better people.

We are glad that you are finally Home.

See ya on the other side.

Love,

Dad

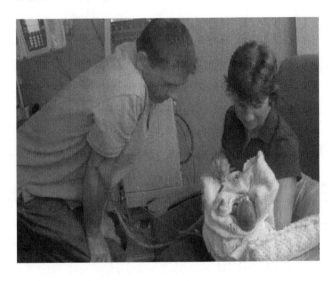

Saturday, April 3, 2010

Pam,

I would like to share some thoughts if you would indulge me. For you the reading might be boring, but for me the writing is therapeutic.

It is difficult to believe that Brooke is gone. From birth to burial she was only with us for 40 days. A lot transpired during those days. A lot of the details of the "ride" I have already shared with you. Many of the lessons, or impressions, feel trapped in my mind. Bear with me as I release some of them.

BE TRUE TO YOUR CONVICTIONS.

When Beck's water broke we were "encouraged" to terminate the pregnancy. Speculation was that something was wrong with the baby. The hospital offered what they deemed to be the "easy way out".

We chose life. God is the author of life. We are created in His image. He makes no mistakes.

Our decision to stay the course was not based upon "quality of life" or convenience, but rather upon our conviction of the sanctity of human life.

Little did we realize that our baby would be used to "save" my wife's life!

When Brooke was born we were again given the option of "letting her pass" or allowing the NICU team to work with her. When we said we wanted them to hand her to the team waiting outside the door, they asked if we were sure.

Based on their computation Brooke was one-day shy of being "viable". With a soft yes and a gentle nod we started Brooke's "ride".

We have no regrets. If we had violated our convictions, we would have no peace.

TAKE EVERY THOUGHT CAPTIVE.

As you are aware, on Saturday we were able to hold Brooke for the first time and gather together with our whole family. It was a "mountaintop" experience.

Late in the day Dr. K. came to the room and asked if she could speak to me in the hallway (reminded me of school). She wanted permission to do an autopsy on Brooke. Not the decision I wanted to be confronted with when holding my daughter for the first time. A seed was cast.

I tried to avert it by thanking Dr. K. for everything they did for Brooke and commented on how difficult it must be to lose a baby. Her response was that what we were going through was rather "rare". She told me that 97% of their babies go home.

A whole handful of seeds were now cast into the wind.
Anger. Bitterness. Jealousy. Self-pity. (You didn't know I was capable did you?). Immediately I had to try to gather these seeds before they took root. Instead of nurturing Satan's seeds, I praised God for the time we had with

Brooke. I thanked him that most families did not have to experience the pain that we were faced with. I went back into the room with my family and left the seeds out in the hallway. We must be careful when opening the doorway of our minds. Not all thoughts are welcome.

Those are the thoughts for today. There are others still waiting to be released. I'm just setting "some" of the captives free. I will probably need more "therapy" in the future. Thanks for indulging me.
Scott

P.S. Does this combination make me a convicted prisoner or a true thinker?

Easter Sunday, April 4, 2010

Pam,

There are some impressions that are just beyond words. Witnessing Brooke pass in Beck's arms, watching the family clean Brooke's body after her passing, handing the undertaker Brooke's dress that her sisters purchased to bring her home in, seeing the backhoe come to dig your daughter's grave, seeing your child's casket suspended over the freshly dug grave, walking up to your children standing over their little sister's grave the evening of her burial, seeing the flower that Brooke's sister's "planted" at the head of her grave, watching Rachel (9 yrs.) run to the cemetery with a bottle of water to care for the flower they "planted".

Rachel approached me a couple of days ago and told me I was right about something (a first). I asked her what she was referring to and she reminded me that I told her that only God can make a person happy. She said she was trying to make herself happy and nothing worked. This is a good reminder for all of us. Joy is a gift. It is a by-product of our relationship with God. Anything we try to manufacture is fleeting. Rachel was trying to create happiness by "doing" something (video game). As I mentioned yesterday, we have to be careful of the thoughts we entertain. Like the rest of our family, Rachel's young mind has been dominated with Brooke's passing. That is only inevitable. Brooke has "consumed" our lives recently. We would not have wanted it any other way. Now we have to shift from all of the anticipation and expectations we had. We have to keep things in an eternal perspective. We have to saturate our minds with the TRUTH. We have to practice Philippians 4:8-9. "Finally, brothers, whatever is true, whatever is noble, whatever is right, whatever is pure, whatever is lovely, whatever is admirable-if anything is excellent or praiseworthy-THINK about such things. Whatever you have learned or received or heard from me, or seen in me-put it into practice. And the God of peace will be with you".

Rachel told Beck that she believes that every time something sad happens, we lose a piece of our heart. BUT, once we get to heaven, we will have a new heart. I love the theology of a 9 year old!!

As Beck and I walked into the cemetery for Brooke's service I told Beck that we have a choice to make. We can either allow the grave to win, or allow the resurrection. We can see Brooke's grave from our bedroom window. When we work in the yard or leave the driveway we can see it. When we walk or run the reminder is there to confront us. Do we allow the sadness of Brooke's death to overwhelm us, or the joy of Christ's resurrection? I'll choose the resurrection!

"Since, then, you have been raised with Christ, set your hearts on things above, where Christ is seated at the right hand of God. Set your minds on things above, not on earthly things. For you died, and

your life is now hidden with Christ in God. When Christ, who is your Life, appears, then you also will appear with Him in glory".
Colossians 3:1-4.

Some impressions are beyond words; some words leave an indelible impression.

"Christ has indeed been raised from the dead, the first-fruits of those who have fallen asleep...The body that is sown is perishable, it is raised imperishable; it is sown in dishonor, it is raised in glory; it is sown in weakness, it is raised in power; it

is sown a natural body, it is raised a spiritual body...Death has been swallowed up in victory. Where, O death is your victory? Where, O death, is your sting?....Thanks be to God! He gives us the victory through our Lord Jesus Christ." May you "experience" the joy of an empty grave this Easter.

Scott

April 16, 2010

Pam,

I mentioned that there were some "impressions" that I wanted to share, sorry for the delay, but tax season sort of got in the way. When we went into the infamous "backroom" at the Funeral Home it was difficult to approach the infant casket setting out for display. The emotions were rather overwhelming. There was an eerie "familiarity" about walking up to the casket. I visited Brooke at the NICU unit almost every day of her life. There was a routine in the visits that consisted of the mandatory 3-minute scrub, a short walk to the isolette, and then "peering in" to see Brooke. The visits were made special by the contact time. Placing my hand on her head to console each of us was special. On the days that the top of the isolette were off I had the great pleasure of actually being able to plant a kiss on her head. I will forever cherish these memories. The overwhelming emotions when approaching the casket came from the feeling of being a spectator. Walking up to the casket and envisioning my daughter inside of it reminded me so much of the isolette. I was always on the outside looking in! We traded in one plastic home for another. Part of me so badly wanted to cry out to God and tell Him how unfair this was. Because of Brooke's situation I was forced to play a role that parents were not created for. We knew however, that it was in Brooke's best interest to be in the care of the Specialists, Mom & Dad would have to wait their turn. As you know, our "turn" never came. At least not with Brooke. While I was wanting to cry out to God, He was whispering to me in that still small voice, "You have 4 other children at home, to what degree are you a spectator in their lives?" Ouch. He always has a way of putting an end to the start of a great pity party!!! I was denied the privilege of being an **active participant** in Brooke's life because of circumstances, but I often *choose* to be a spectator with my other children because of selfishness. How easy it is to allow other people or things (t.v.) to raise our children. I could quote Bible passages about child rearing or give illustrations of the various surrogates we allow to take our place as parents to our children, but I will spare you. Instead I will resolve to be more active in the lives of my children and hope others are encouraged to do the same. I don't ever want that awful feeling of being on the outside looking in, instead I want to have more memories that I can cherish with my children.

Scott

April 26, 2010

Pam,

Today I want to share a fear and a question. As you know, the last couple of months our lives have been filled with a lot of stress, brokenness, & uncertainty. I know it will sound like a paradox, but our lives have also been filled with Peace, Joy & Truth. When I was faced with the prospect of losing both Beck & Brooke, for a short period of time a felt like I was "on an island". I was faced with many decisions as two medical teams were coming to me with questions, info, and requests for signatures (release forms, not autographs). It was definitely more than I could handle, which is precisely where God wanted me. I was "forced", with baby steps at first, to walk hand in hand with God. A lot of tears were shed, but in the midst of the storm, I learned that in God's hands we cannot be harmed. The furnace of affliction is a great place to be "purified".

Brooke is now gone, Beck is "out of the woods", and I am back into life's routines. I think you know by now what my fear is. I cannot fabricate the furnace or manufacture the heat, but I am afraid of "losing" the incredible intimacy that is experienced in brokenness. There is something refreshing about being transparent before and dependent upon others as we grow in faith together. I guess my fear is becoming "cold" outside of the furnace. Obviously the fear leads to the question: How? How to "maintain" the intimate walk when life is "more comfortable". Perhaps those that followed the updates and "joined" the ride may be experiencing some of the same feelings. I wonder how many have maintained the "interest" or should I say the spiritual fervor now that the journey is currently more "stable"? Are the prayers as fervent or consistent? How many are still "crying out" to God on a regular basis? Somehow we have to recognize that we are all desperate. We all need to be transparent. You need my prayers just as much as I have needed and continue to need yours. I certainly don't have all the answers but I believe that we all need to learn to appropriate the Truth that we know and as we do God will "reveal" or "illuminate" even more to us. There seems to be a big gap between "knowing" and experiencing. We were created for fellowship with God, can we have the intimacy without the furnace? If not my sympathies go out to those who never experienced the "heat". It is truly a walk you will never forget. I am not trying to be condescending, but I hope to encourage you and give God the glory He deserves. As I have stated before He has been so faithful to us during this trial, I would be remiss not to share it. I hope our time "in the furnace" encourages everyone to pursue a deeper relationship with God through Christ, our Savior who was acquainted with pain, suffering and sorrow. Thanks for letting me share the ramblings. If you know the answer to the million-dollar question, please let me know!!

Scott

A letter to Brooke from Daddy

Brooke,

There are so many things I wanted to share with you but time would not allow. First and foremost, I wanted to share my love. I wanted you to know how precious you are; created in the image of God. I wanted to hold you and tickle you and teach you about Jesus. I wanted to hear your voice and I wanted to hear you giggle. I wanted to celebrate your first birthday and many more besides. I wanted to see you interact with your siblings; I wanted to see you rocked by your mother. I wanted to push you in the swing and take you for walks with your little hand in mine.

I wanted to rest with you sleeping on my chest. I wanted to take you to the cottage or the beach and watch you splash in the water or play in the sand. I wanted to see your expression the first time you ate ice cream. I wanted to see you ride a bike. I wanted to pick you up when you fell down. I wanted to hear you say "mommy" and "daddy". I wanted to watch you play with dolls. I wanted to see you in your cute little dresses. I wanted to see you play in the snow and sled down the hills. I wanted to pray with you with your little hand in mine. I wanted to see you drive (sort of), and grow in independence. I wanted to see you grow in humility, and truly learn to be dependent. I wanted to help you with your math, (after you squirmed for a while). I wanted to watch you play sports or play an instrument. I wanted to listen to music with you and have talks with you. I wanted to take you hunting and fishing and spend time outdoors with you. I wanted to see your expression at Christmas. I wanted to see how you would handle adversity, and more importantly, how you would handle success. I wanted to walk you down the aisle with your "little" hand in mind.

The most important thing I wanted was for you to bring glory to God. Although your time was short, you gave me what I wanted most. Your little feet left large footprints. Your courageous fight united many people. You reminded us of the power of prayer and the importance of faith. You also reminded us that all life is worth fighting for. You brought out the best in people. You reminded me that this earth is not my home and that I am just a steward, even of "my" children. You reminded me that love never fails.

Never. With your little hand in mine you helped me to embrace the cross like never before.

Thank you for sharing your love with me.

I love you.

Daddy

P.S. It is comforting to know that your little hands are now in the hands of Jesus.

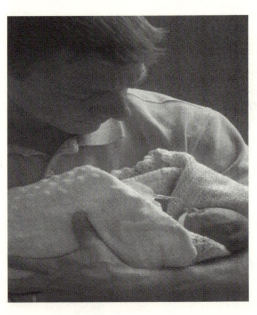

Seven years have come and gone since Brooke's passing. Tears are still shed and questions are still asked. What would her personality be like? How would she interact with her siblings and nieces and nephew? It's hard to see little girls about her age without asking these and numerous other questions. One question we don't ask is: Why us? Self-pity is not an option. Sympathy is of no benefit.

We do not question the Sovereignty of God. To live with doubts or despair is to imply that this world is all there is. It is not. We have more than memories of Brooke's short life. We have hope. We believe that we will be reunited with

Brooke someday for all of eternity. Keeps things in perspective. All of our lives are a mist. We try not to cling too tightly to the things of the world. The things that are most valuable are Heaven sent, appreciate them while you have them. And don't forget to hug them!! Thanks for sharing Brooke's journey. And don't forget, it's the Destination that ultimately counts.

Thank you so much for reading this book! My desire is to reach as many people as I can with encouraging material. If you could help me with that by leaving an amazon review, I would greatly appreciate it.

Made in the USA
Columbia, SC
31 October 2023